Dear Parent:
Your child's love of reading starts here!

Every child learns to read in a different way and at his or her own speed. Some go back and forth between reading levels and read favorite books again and again. Others read through each level in order. You can help your young reader improve and become more confident by encouraging his or her own interests and abilities. From books your child reads with you to the first books he or she reads alone, there are I Can Read Books for every stage of reading:

SHARED READING
Basic language, word repetition, and whimsical illustrations, ideal for sharing with your emergent reader

BEGINNING READING
Short sentences, familiar words, and simple concepts for children eager to read on their own

READING WITH HELP
Engaging stories, longer sentences, and language play for developing readers

READING ALONE
Complex plots, challenging vocabulary, and high-interest topics for the independent reader

ADVANCED READING
Short paragraphs, chapters, and exciting themes for the perfect bridge to chapter books

I Can Read Books have introduced children to the joy of reading since 1957. Featuring award-winning authors and illustrators and a fabulous cast of beloved characters, I Can Read Books set the standard for beginning readers.

A lifetime of discovery begins with the magical words **"I Can Read!"**

Visit www.icanread.com for information
on enriching your child's reading experience.

I Can Read Book® is a trademark of HarperCollins Publishers.

Alvin and the Chipmunks: Alvin and the Big Art Show
Alvin and the Chipmunks Motion Picture © 2014 Twentieth Century Fox Film Corporation and Regency Entertainment (USA), Inc. in the U.S. only.
© 2014 Twentieth Century Fox Film Corporation and Monarchy Enterprises S.a.r.l. in all other territories.
Alvin and The Chipmunks, The Chipettes, and Characters TM & © 2014 Bagdasarian Productions, LLC. All rights reserved.
Manufactured in China.

ISBN 978-0-06-225225-8
Typography by Rick Farley

14 15 16 17   SCP   10 9 8 7 6 5 4 3 2

First Edition

I Can Read!

READING
2
WITH HELP

ALVIN
AND THE CHIPMUNKS

Alvin and the Big Art Show

By Jodi Huelin
Illustrations by Artful Doodlers

HARPER
An Imprint of HarperCollinsPublishers

The boys were getting ready

for the school art show.

Parents and students came.

Even the teachers and principal came.

It was a big deal.

Simon was excited.

He was reading a book on Pablo Picasso.

He was making a self-portrait.

Theodore was excited, too.

He was very proud of his project.

"I'd rather be skateboarding," Alvin said.

"But since I'm here, let's make some art!"

He was using the clay wheel.

Really, he was making a huge mess!

Theodore worked very hard.

He hoped to win the blue ribbon

for Best Sculpture.

"Do I have a chance?" he asked.

"A chance for what?" asked Alvin,

flicking clay all over.

Theodore sighed at his brother.

Simon rolled his eyes.

Maybe Alvin

should have been skateboarding.

He was covered in clay!

Before long, art class was over.

Theodore was sad to leave.

He was sure his project

would be the art show's first

and only drum set made of paper.

Theodore thought
about his drum set all day.
He even wanted to skip lunch.
"But it's Taco Tuesday!" Alvin said.
"On second thought, my project
can wait!" Theodore said.

The next day in class, Theodore's

teacher praised her star student.

"Keep exploring your artistic self!"

Mrs. Harris said.

Theodore smiled.

Alvin wasn't happy with his project.

He wouldn't win a ribbon.

He was bored.

He wanted something fun to do.

"Come on, Alvin. I'll help you,"

Theodore said.

But Alvin wasn't interested

in making art.

He wanted to make some music.

First, Alvin began to sing.

Then he began to dance.

He shook to the left.

Then he shook to the right.

He played air guitar.

Alvin danced around,

knocking over paints and brushes.

He bumped right into . . .

Theodore's art project!

"Alvin!" Theodore yelled.

A cymbal had crashed

into the bass drum

and made a huge hole.

"I'm so sorry!" Alvin said.

But Theodore didn't want to hear it.

He knew his brother was bored.

He knew his brother

didn't care about the art show.

"My project is ruined!" Theodore cried.

Theodore was so upset he ran

out of the room.

Just then the bell rang.

School was over for the day.

Theodore ran all the way home.

Simon looked at Alvin.

"What are you going to do?" he asked.

"You broke Theodore's project."

Alvin knew there was only one

thing to do: he had to fix it.

The rest of the class left.

Some headed to after-school clubs.

Some headed to soccer practice.

Alvin wasn't going anywhere.

He had work to do.

"Please, Mrs. Harris!" Alvin begged.

He had to learn how to make paper drums.

He rolled up his sleeves.

Mrs. Harris brought strips of newspaper,

buckets of glue, and cups of water.

Alvin got a crash course in paper sculpture.

He set to work and did his best.

Simon was impressed.

His brother was focused and determined.

Simon decided to help, too.

When they got home they were tired
and they were hungry.

"Hi, boys, let's eat!" Dave said.

Alvin was surprised.

Theodore hadn't told Dave.

But Theodore ignored Alvin all night.

He did his homework in silence.

He brushed his teeth in silence.

"Good night, Theodore," said Alvin.

Theodore didn't say anything back.

"Are you ready for the show tonight?"

Dave asked the next morning.

"I can't wait to see your drum set!"

Theodore smiled sadly.

He headed out to the bus stop alone.

Theodore avoided the art room

until it was time for class.

He went into the room

and put his head on the table.

"What's wrong?" Mrs. Harris asked.

"Aren't you excited for the show?"

"How could I . . ." Theodore started.

He turned toward Mrs. Harris.

And there she stood, in front of his drums.

They had been fixed.

They were perfect!

"What happened?" Theodore asked.

He didn't understand.

When he left yesterday

the art project was destroyed.

Now it was even better than before.

"Ask your brothers," Mrs. Harris said.

"I'm sorry I broke your drums," Alvin said.

"I'm sorry you were upset," said Simon.

"But we fixed them!" Alvin said.

Theodore smiled.

That night, Alvin, Simon,

and Theodore went to the art show.

Dave was there, too.

"The drums are amazing!" Dave said.

"You're a great artist!"

"Actually, we're *all* great artists,"

Theodore said.

"I couldn't have done it

without my brothers."

After the show, the boys went
out for ice cream to celebrate.
And Theodore wore his
first-place ribbon.